DAILY INFUSIONS

Books by Gary Hewins

Daily Infusions Series
(devotional series)

Book 1: *Discovering Your Fullness in Christ*
Book 2: *Behold!*
Book 3: *About the Father's Business*

Other Titles

Truth Serum: America's Ever-Increasing Need for Pulpiteers (2017)

DAILY INFUSIONS

About the Father's Business

Dr. Gary Hewins

Daily Infusions

Book 3

Daily Infusions: About the Father's Business
Dr. Gary Hewins

Publisher: Lifepoints at Five Apple Farm
www.Lifepoints.life

ISBN-13: 979-8-9993207-0-4

in·fu·sion / in-ˈfyü-zhən /

Transfusions, by definition, introduce a like element (e.g. blood) into a system to simply increase that element's volume and pressure to achieve a required physiological norm.

Infusions, by definition, introduce an entirely different element into a system to alter its level of vitality and purpose, often with redemptive, restorative, and therapeutic results.

Infuse water with your favorite tea leaves and simply wait as it steeps to alter your afternoon experience of restoration and reflection.

Infuse your bank account with capital and satisfy financial obligations, consider an exotic vacation, and explore the joys of generosity.

Infuse your body, soul, and spirit with the following "infusions" of truth and enjoy an increased volume of the Spirit, an ever-growing appetite for Christ, and invigorating moments of restoration and readiness. The following daily "treatments" will alter your level of spiritual vitality as you discover your fullness in Christ. These are not long-shot experimental treatments but tried-and-true daily infusions based on the immovable promises of God, which are "yes" and "amen" in Christ.

Seek the LORD and his strength; seek his presence continually!
1 Chronicles 16:11 (ESV)

Pastor Gary

Table of Contents

Introduction

Members of today's workforce labor daily to produce the greatest economy in the world. From the mailroom to the boardroom, today's marketplace is stocked with hopeful upstarts and experienced experts, all inspired to prosper with unprecedented capitalistic savvy. Corporate ladders provide our nation a means to climb to new and innovative heights. Globalization keeps us highly competitive and, far too often, ruthless.

What would happen if our secular marketplace were increasingly infused with spiritual power, insight, efficiency, and intentionality? What if the believing executive continued the pursuit of a fine career in the form of a divine calling? What if there existed an infusion of daily power and discernment that raised established bottom lines, created new opportunities, and advanced innovation for the future?

Market-wide change takes place through a multitude of personal changes. In the pages ahead, today's worker can enjoy even greater results in the marketplace through the merger of the laborer with the Spirit of the Living God, Who is always about the Father's business.

As you read the following daily infusions, you will quickly notice that each day's title ends with "-ous." The meaning of this suffix is "to be made full of;" it creates a descriptive adjective from an otherwise informative noun.

Prosperity is great, but to be "prosper*ous*" is to live a life full of prosperity. Generosity is a wonderful thing, but to actually be "gener*ous*" infers a life infused with generosity. "Ferocity" is a great noun, but to be "feroci*ous*" connotes a life or career filled with strength, passion, and tenacity.

The following *Daily Infusions* and the brief prayers that follow them are simply a means of jumpstarting a daily habit of filling yourself with the truth of God's Word. The Spirit of God is the Infuser. He is the Filler. He wishes to infuse you with everything good for doing good in the marketplace and in life.

And the disciples were filled with joy and with the Holy Spirit (Acts 13:52).

———————————

Lord, whenever and wherever I labor apart from Your insight, wisdom, and prudence, take me to a Rock that is higher than I. Show me how to masterfully conduct business at a much higher level of efficiency, fruitfulness, and enjoyment. Move in me, that I in turn might move others. Infuse me daily, that I may dream of and surely see a spiritual awakening in this marketplace that will yield spiritual dividends for generations to come.

Amen.

DAY 1
Intraven*ous*

To them God has chosen to make known among the Gentiles the glorious riches of this mystery, which is Christ in you, the hope of glory.
Colossians 1:27

You know how to set the tone and trajectory for your workday. Before the "open" sign is hung, before the market bell is rung, before you enter the subway or your cubicle, before class begins, before your first meeting, before the conveyor belt starts, or before you see your first patient, client, or customer, you know the need for "infusion."

The Spirit of God is your spiritual IV, infusing every part of you with everything you need to labor today in the name of Christ. In your business, you are mindful of the Father's business. You remain ready and on point to work, lead, follow, and serve...but you must freely receive before you can freely give. Ask Him for such a day-starting infusion.

In Christ, you are infused with divine strength and insight to meet the vocational demands of your day. His Word is your spiritual supplement, readying you to make wise decisions, set clear priorities, reach goals, and influence others. You are afforded the privilege of working in tandem with your Lord, and you've learned that His yoke is far easier than yours. He is your intravenous infusion of clarity protecting you from the dangers of busyness while centering you in the joy of productivity. You are being strengthened to meet and exceed the responsibilities entrusted to you. You are more than capable; your capability is rivaled only by your faithfulness. In fact, because you have been faithful in the little things, He is giving you charge over many things. You are a humble team player, solving problems and resolving conflicts. You foster prosperity and success for yourself, for others, and for the kingdom. You may work for another, but you first labor for Him. Whatever you do today, do it as unto Him. He is your ultimate promoter. Promote Him in word and in deed. Exemplify truth and excellence, and He will promote you.

You are a producer. You are infused with all that is needed to labor in your discipline while laboring in love. You are equipped for every good work. You are infused with brilliance, creativity, wisdom, and giftedness. You "work smart" when working hard is insufficient. You see things others cannot see and do things others have yet to even consider. Truth is your road map to treasure, and you are a prospering steward of abundance. In Christ, you are not common, but extraordinary.

When you were hired, He was hired, too. He came with you. He is in you, the hope of glory. You are infused with Him, set apart to be exemplary. You are now, and will remain, highly profitable and highly prophet-able in the workplace. Wherever you go today, be fully present, attentive, dutiful, and sensitive to the needs of others. You are infused with the power of effectiveness to do even greater works than Christ. No demand or challenge today can or will overtake you. You are both infused and sealed. Enjoy His partnership with you today. Your countenance will display your joy before others.

Others will look to you for guidance, regardless of your position or lack thereof.

You are a blood-bought child of the King. His lifeblood courses through your veins. Serve Him in the marketplace today until the "closed" sign is hung, until the market's closing bell rings, until you leave your cubicle or return on the subway. Serve Him diligently through your labor until the last meeting adjourns, the conveyor belt halts, or until you have seen your last patient, client, or customer. Then allow His "IV infusion" to help you rest and enjoy the many ways He continually blesses you. Well done.

Infuse me today, Lord, to levels deep within me. I desire You in my deepest thoughts, my biggest dreams, and the deepest marrow of who I am and will be. I want and need spiritual depth. Infuse me with that depth and privilege me to make a deeper impact on others in your Name.

Amen.

DAY 2
Glorious

And whatever you do in word or deed,
do all in the name of the Lord Jesus,
giving thanks to God the Father through Him.
Colossians 3:17 (ESV)

Regardless of the color of your collar, work is worship. Work is worship, and you love to gloriously worship. Your zeal for work reflects your zeal for the Lord. If you do not work, you do not eat, for you must worship your Provider. You are a fruitful worker; thus, you are a fruitful worshiper. You worship Him today with your hands, your mind, your back, and your shoulders; you worship Him with your knowledge and your experience. Your persistence honors Him; your diligence and discipline, too. How glorious is your labor before the Lord! You work not for earthly masters, but for the Divine Godhead. Whatever you do, you do as unto the Lord.

Worship Him in spirit and in truth and dispense the full arsenal of your giftedness as an expression of worship. You eagerly desire spiritual gifts because you eagerly desire to use them to worship. He fans into flame the gifts He has planted in you. You use what He has given you to give back to Him your expressions of worship. You are specifically gifted in unique and personal ways to worship person-ally and intimately through those gifts. You are skilled and gifted in the marketplace. You are becoming an artist or artisan in your vocational harvest field. You are both His craftsmanship and His anointed craftsman. The way you work is worshipful. When your work is worshipful, your work is anointed.

You sing and make melody in your heart to the Lord, and in your pursuit of excellence in your work, you make glorious overtures to Him. You aim for perfection in work, for He is perfect in every way. The more your work becomes worship, the less you fatigue; conversely, the more selfish your labor, the more weary you become. You are a worshiper in the marketplace. In the realm of commerce, you exalt Him in word and in deed. While others seek to secure manna, you worship the One who provides it. You are different. You are anointed to work with all your heart, as unto Him.

Your entire paradigm of work is morphing and intensifying even now. As your work becomes a fragrant offering to the Lord, you yourself are raised up. Your humility exalts you. You ascend not only a corporate ladder, but Jacob's ladder. The deeper your worship, the broader your influence. You love Him with all your heart, and you work using that same heart as an instrument of worship. Your work/worship is now fresh and living. You work in a new and living way. Work is now uplifting, magnifying, necessary, energizing, purposeful, and appreciated. How glorious is your worship before the throne as you labor in the power of His name! You work in His sight and within His reach, and you invite Him into your labor; you collaborate with the Divine. You make coin, but you also enjoy the koinonia.

You worship Him as you serve, sell, distribute, train, consult, manufacture, assemble, transport, and dispense your duties as an ambassador of Christ. You worship through working, and it is increasingly glorious and liberating. Your smile is worshipful. You slay the most hardened heart with kindness. Your attitude is celebratory, for today you work as unto the Lord.

You have work; therefore, you have a vehicle by which to worship. Whatever your vocation, whatever your location, you are being compensated to worship the Lord through your labor. Your worshipful work produces more than the work of those who labor only for themselves. He inhabits the praises of His people, and you choose to praise Him in and through your work.

Your work is worship. The Spirit of God inhabits your career and remains mindful of your glorious, worshipful work.

Father, I ask nothing of You today but an opportunity to bless You. Today, I worship You in spirit and in truth. I worship You with my lips, my body, my work, and my body of work. I magnify You today, and as I do, my challenges will grow smaller. I love You, my King.
Amen.

DAY 3
Infectious

Look carefully then how you walk, not as unwise but as wise, making the best use of the time, because the days are evil. Therefore do not be foolish, but understand what the will of the Lord is.
Ephesians 5:15–16 (ESV)

You can handle tough assignments and daunting tasks. Some uncomfortable, seemingly impossible tasks can become intimidating, scary monsters when left to linger for days, if not weeks, on a long to-do list. These challenging responsibilities can swell into vocation-al infections, festering and swelling into putrid, fetid, career hindering gangrene. Many procrastinate; you do not. You are infused by your Maker to overcome the most daunting and seemingly formidable tasks before you. You tackle the most difficult tasks first, not last, and never not at all. You dispatch difficult things early so worry will not weigh on you into the night.

Your discipline liberates you from the entanglements of a dazed idleness. You are quick to conquer what only appears to be capable of conquering you. You are an overcomer. You do not have a spirit of timidity. You face difficult tasks. You face difficult people. You face difficult situations. You have

10

a greater fear of the Lord than you do of man. You make difficult calls and engage in difficult conversations. You confront what others dread but cannot seem to face.

The Spirit in you counsels you as you move through difficulties instead of around them. You overcome adversity in a timely manner. You function with confidence and boldness and, consequently, you are bound by nothing. No difficult task controls you, defines you, pesters you, or thwarts your worship. Nothing stymies your worshipful work. You are mature, even beyond your years. You deal with what needs to be dealt with, employing dignity, resolve, and transparency. You are resolute.

In the power of your own flesh, sepsis ensues, but in Christ, any difficulty can be handled. The Spirit of God works with you; He works within you, and He works through you. You are hemmed in on all sides by the divine assistance you need to be victorious. He is your promised help, and His promises are "yes" and "amen" in Christ. You can do all things through Christ who strengthens you. He is established in you; thus, you are established. He is holy; thus, you remain whole, intact, pure. He holds all things together. When others are falling apart, you remain unbroken. Simply ask for and anticipate the insight and fortitude to handle difficult situations as they arise.

Challenges sit perched atop your to-do list, only to be toppled over early. Many victories come early for you because you are fearless. When necessary, you will take action as the Lord leads you, not as your flesh delays. When you wait on the Lord, you find renewed strength. When you wait on your own flesh to acquire the needed gumption to act, your strength withers.

Your Lord dealt with challenges and overcame them. He who lives in you is helping you overcome, as well. No weapon formed against you will ever prosper. You will overcome by the power of the blood of the Lamb and the word of your testimony. Fear not. He is able. Deal now with what must be dealt with, and He will impart the necessary tact, wisdom, and resourcefulness to finish the task well.

Your challenges only appear daunting. Be not deceived. You are discerning, credible, wise like a serpent and gentle like a dove. What can waylay you in the Spirit? Do you not love Him? Does perfect love not cast out fear? Make the call now. Set up the meeting now. Deal with the issue now. Address the financial matter now. Communicate. Discuss. Correct. Make a change. Now. Tomorrow has enough worries of its own. Destroy the intimidating façade of your least-liked task. Break it down, deal with it, and overcome.

Whatever you focus on in life will certainly enlarge. Fix your eyes on Him. Take your eyes off the task. Magnify Him and shrink your challenge. You are Christ-oriented. You are results-oriented. You are people-oriented. Rise up and allow Him to take you to a rock higher than yourself.

Lord, surely there is something of You in me that is to be evident to others. Make the "You" in me contagious. May those around me become warmer to, if not feverish for, Christ.
Amen.

DAY 4
Ingeni*ous*

For "who has known the mind of the LORD that he may instruct Him?" But we have the mind of Christ.
1 Corinthians 2:16 (NKJV)

You are creative. You have access to creativity. You are far more creative than you can fathom. You know your Creator. You serve the Source of all creation and creativity. Creativity is not a personality strength or a personality limitation; He is your creativity. He has ingeniously prepared your sanctified mind with innovation, rethinking, resolving, and replenishing.

You have access to the mind of Christ. You are a thinker who believes and a believer who thinks. Ponder and dream away. Consider things not yet considered. Explore the depths of solutions inaccessible to multitudes of others. Your God-given childlike curiosity leads you to solutions and remedies for situations and for people. You have within you The Genius—not just *a* genius, but *the* tender-hearted, merciful, and compassionate Genius who desires for you to help even the least of those among us.

You can and will figure out solutions to challenges in the marketplace, in the world, in your God-given sphere of influence. Never belittle your own ability to tap into His vast capability. Only you can limit His brilliant voice, His brilliant thoughts, His brilliant instructions. You are finite, but in Him, you have infinite possibilities. You are an asset to any company, organization, or institution, for you are wise enough to not just seek answers but to seek the One who has them.

You are capable in Christ. Only you can limit your own potential. All things are possible. The only ignorance you possess is rooted in ignoring Him, your Creator. Your passion, coupled with His mind, is a dangerously productive combination. When you were hired, so too was your Lord.

You are compensated, but His wisdom and direction remain priceless.

Be infused today with understanding. Be infused this workday with curiosity. Be infused today with profound insight. Ignore Him and be ignorant. Seek Him and solve problems. Be quickened by the mind of Christ. Practice His presence and, in so doing, think like He thinks. Because you are growing in wisdom, you are growing in stature in Christ.

Begin to think clearer. Think not *like* Christ; think *with* Christ. Be infused with divine processing, divine logic, divine reasoning. Let Him elevate your ideas. Elevate your thoughts. Elevate your expectations. Elevate your opinion of your capacity to partner with Him. Grow far away from under-estimating divine intervention. He is your glory and the lifter of your head, your thinking, your being, your status, and your lot in life. You are a Christ-centered, Spirit-dependent student of truth, sold out to a divine calling to overcome sin and redeem situations that leave people empty, lonely, and hopeless.

Work at this with all your heart, but also love Him with all of your creative, innovative, and ingenious mind. You are brilliant in Christ. You are revelatory in Christ. Just think: you have access to the mind of Christ, the thoughts of Christ, the teachings of Christ, the commandments of Christ, and the prayers of Christ. Through the power of the Spirit, you can enter into the ponderings and motivations of Christ in his *logos*, His Word.

You are reasonable. In fact, you can reason with God and reason with others. You will articulate truth in ways that leave others speechless. Christ's brilliance through you will be dumbfounding to others. You are sharp, keen, clear, and settled into the meditations and ruminations of Jesus, the risen Lord. It is only right—and righteous—that you think more highly of yourself, for in Christ, you are a treasured gem, an invaluable employee, partner, cohort, associate.

Think on these things and raise the bar of mediocrity to a new and living divine standard. You are fully engaged and fully alive in Christ. You are a human being first and a human doing second. Get your daily infusion of ingenuity, for the glory of God.

Father, by faith, quicken my thoughts. Help me to do as You have done; help me care for others as You have cared for me. Help me solve problems, create solutions, and process thoughts beyond my own ability. Keep me sharp, alive, and sensitive to Your Spirit.

Amen.

DAY 5
Studi*ous*

"But blessed are your eyes for they see, and your ears for they hear; for assuredly, I say to you that many prophets and righteous men desired to see what you see, and did not see it, and to hear what you hear, and did not hear it."
Matthew 13:16–17 (NKJV)

You are a student of truth and a student of people. You are anointed by God to be attentive. You can listen like a blind man listens. Sight, for you, can actually be a secondary sense. You hear both spoken words and unspoken sentiments. You are an artistic, gifted listener. You can hear pain. You can listen with your ears, using their delicate and intricate physiology, but you can also listen with your heart and your belly. The compassion in you can actually hear. You can hear a "yes" when others hear a "no." You can hear a "no" when others hear a "yes." You are discerning.

You are prosperous in life and in the marketplace because you listen. Some hear and forget. You listen and apply. You have a radar for truth and a desire to hear and heed quality instruction. People can see and sense your attentiveness. Your adeptness of understanding is only rivaled by your willingness to adapt. You help people because you are among the few who hear their hearts. You place people over products;

you minister to people first, and your service or product is second. You care authentically. Silence is not a foe. You are considerate. You patiently wait as you actively listen. You talk over no one. You interrupt no one—especially your Lord.

You used to operate at a pace that fostered chaos and distraction. You now live with an intentionality that fosters focus. You are a methodical, caring, sensitive listener. You are single-minded, stable, and pure in heart. Wherever you are, you are fully present. You give precedence to truly hearing what your customers, superiors, and fellow workers are saying. You are exceptionally equipped to help others prosper. Your faith comes by hearing, and hearing by the Word of God. You have great faith not just because you see truth, but because you also hear truth. You study and listen.

You are a studious observer. You see detail. You see things and people in a way others don't see them. You can see behind a person's mask. You can see when people lower their guard, and you can watch their trust go up. You are no casual spectator. You are a skilled, caring witness. Your observations add value to people. You will not see a project until you see the person. You are personable, amiable, and genuinely interested in others. You are not about slick sales techniques; you are about real people, real needs, and real results. Yes, you are highly observant, but not passively so. Your observations earn you merited respect. Your active observations and your active listening yield active trust in the marketplace. You are a great exception in a world that is hurried and harried. You do more with less than others do with seemingly endless opportunities.

You are a student of authority. You study to be an authority in your field. You study to acquire needed expertise. Your listening and observation skills provide for a mantle of authority. Because you listen, you are heard. Because you observe, people look to you with respect. You understand authority and the need to submit to it. Your humility earns you respect. You are exalted in your field because you humble yourself in the sight of God and man.

You are certainly studious. You know the importance of learning but, more importantly, you know how to learn. You know the importance of listening over the value of hearing yourself speak. You know that your expertise is less important than remaining teachable.

You are prospering. You will continue to prosper as your work remains worshipful and you remain a student and disciple of your Lord Jesus.

You are my favorite professor, Lord. Teach me, for Your servant is listening. Instruct me today that I may profess You in word and in deed. I am sitting at Your feet, ready to be taught and ready to obey You in love.

Amen.

DAY 6
Gener*ous*

"Give, and it will be given to you. Good measure, pressed down, shaken together, running over, will be put into your lap. For with the measure you use it will be measured back to you."
Luke 6:38 (ESV)

Your work, in part, is the means by which your Lord resources your needs, fulfills your wants, and funds your dreams. When an accounting of your life comes to pass, you will be appreciated as one who has found joy in generosity. Some concern themselves with rising interest rates, but you have a rising interest in being generous. You are never more like Christ than when you give, for God so loved the world that He gave.

You are a blessed conduit of resources. You are gifted to give. Giving to others is for you a privilege. You do not give to get; as such, you are a cheerful giver. You have a need to be generous just like you have a need to worship—without either in your life, you cease to be you, and you slowly cease to know yourself. You know you were redeemed to give.

You are generous with your time. You are aware that money is no replacement for time. There are those in your life who truly need time with you. Time is not yours to give, but it is yours to share. You generously share your time with others. You do not spend time. You do not waste time. You invest time. Time with you betters all parties and yields significant dividends. When sharing time, you share yourself. You share insights and ideas and you also share testimonies of successes and of failures. You are transparent when warranted as you generously share yourself with others. You share encouragement and make deposits of hope. Time is simply the context in which your generosity flourishes. You are efficient in your endeavors, thus utilizing your time to invest in others, in your causes, and in your mission. You see things in ways others do not. You prioritize in ways others do not. You accomplish things others do not. Your generosity is necessary and vital. You understand that should you hoard your gifts and perspectives, your company, your team, and your coworkers will flail about in a sea of selfishness.

You are discerningly generous. Your joyous generosity can be strategically withheld when warranted. You will not enable others on their journey of learning. Your concern for those in your realm of influence is expressed through a tough generosity: you wisely let others learn lessons that last. You recognize when it is prudent to withhold. Lasting lessons may leave scars, but those scars heal over time. To know you is to know one who perceives when to "slow" versus "go." There are those in your life who, even under your supervision, need to learn and experience firsthand the lessons of commerce and work ethics. By allowing them to grow through failing—and then helping them up after they fall—you exhibit a deeper, richer blend of generosity.

Your Lord compensates you as you sit at His desk, under His roof, selling or making His products, using His stapler and sticky notes. You sit before His laptop; you travel on His airplanes to cities He owns. You deposit "your" check in His bank, only to later disperse it to His utility companies, His restaurants, and His babysitters. The earth is the LORD's, and everything in it. Your Lord compensates you to be His conduit of blessing to those who lack resources, meaning, redemption, and identity.

He demonstrated His generosity by paying a debt you could not pay before you even realized you owed it. He gave you time because it was His to give, and He shares that time with you so you, in turn, can experience the joy of generosity. He point-blank asks you to challenge Him to a generosity duel that will only intensify your joy and jubilation. Labor in your harvest field today knowing He is compensating you to care for your own and for those who are aimless and hopeless. He cheers you on to be a cheerful giver.

Father, by this day's end, may I have given more to others than I have received, and may I be fuller and richer for it. Amen.

DAY 7
Prosper*ous*

"You shall remember the LORD your God, for it is he who gives you power to get wealth, that he may confirm his covenant that he swore to your fathers, as it is this day."
Deuteronomy 8:18 (ESV)

You are already prosperous in Christ. You are already seated in heavenly places with every spiritual blessing in Christ. You already have a God who excessively lavishes His love on you. You already worship One who not only meets needs but also sets asides baskets of leftovers. Your excessive, nearly reckless God understands abundance, banquets, and feasting. How excessive can He be? He has already teed up for you the reality of eternity! He is not generous because He is bored. His generosity is not a hobby or something He tinkers with; it is who He is. His generosity just *is*. His nature is to prosper His children. Is it yours? Is His nature within you moving you in directions He Himself would take?

Your response to His generous nature is refreshingly strange. Your deep plea to Him in the wake of a tsunami of blessings is an oddity. When it comes to abundance and prosperity, you know to listen oh so carefully to that soft, muffled whisper within you. Many others do not hear it, as their celebration is too loud. Because you listen, you are peculiar. Your peculiarity denotes an unusual, seldom-seen maturity. Your maturity prepares you to steward an even greater abundance very few ever encounter. Your strange plea is to temporarily hold back the abundance. You are among the few who politely and respectfully ask that the prosperity be delayed. Delayed? Until when?

You want to prioritize the blessing and the freedom it seemingly represents. You are the one making sure you pursue the Blesser first and always, not just the blessing. You are the rare person who wants nothing to come between you and Him. You want to be stripped of any wrong motives, any possessions, anything that would cost you nearness to Christ. You know to take stock of who you are. You want a greater love for your Lord than you want what He can do for you. What He has already done for you is undeservedly excessive. You want nothing to do with the love of money or the shortcuts to acquire it. You want Him near and first—before, during, and after the blessing.

You want to be prepared. To whom much is given, much is required. You do not fear prosperity, only its potential rule over you. You want to glorify God, not glory in abundance. You want Him to remain your Source of security and peace. You want to continue to meditate on His Word day and night so that you will be prosperous and successful. You do not want abundance to cease your meditation and quench your thirst for righteousness.

Yes, you are peculiar, as Christ was peculiar. Your peculiarity is refreshing. You see the necessary, proportional relationship between riches and maturity. Because you see and because you listen, you will be blessed. Work in your field with all your heart, but do not lose your heart in the process. Seek success, but do not fail to acknowledge its true

Source. You are a workman approved. You know to ready yourself for riches, while others do not. They may receive yet waste, but you will receive and retain. You are the steward He seeks. You can be trusted to seek first His kingdom and His righteousness. You are on point; you work hard, work smart, and ready yourself for a windfall that will not cause you to fall. Your awareness and sensitivity may yield you prosperity. As great a blessing as that is, you know it is better to give than to receive.

Lord, if only I could account for the innumerable buckets of blessings You have poured on me! I am prosperous today. Prosper me, too, by enlightening the eyes of my heart to see and sense the deep need others have for hope.
Amen.

DAY 8
Perspicac*ious*

"For which of you, intending to build a tower,
does not sit down first and count the cost,
whether he has enough to finish it..."
Luke 14:28–30 (NKJV)

Christ has a plan to prosper you. He has no plan to harm you. Knowing your past, He has your best in mind—both your present and your future. Yes, Divine Providence gifts you and gives you opportunities. Providence may open doors and secure possibilities and positions, but you know you need more. You are called to work and work smart. Nothing is simply handed to you; you earn what you have. You earn respect, credibility, and money. When coupled with your Lord, you have all you need to prosper a great business partnership.

In Christ, like Christ, you need to devise a plan of action. Confer with Him. You are a planner and a strategist, and you have the acumen necessary for success. You take action, and you know how best to allocate resources. You have more understanding than what is common and expected. You are distinctively uncommon; there-fore, you yield uncommon, unprecedented results.

Before you endeavor to reach your goals and fulfill your calling, you count the cost, time, and resources necessary for success. You finish what you start, and you only start what can be finished. You finish well because you start well and prioritize well. As you lean on and lean into your Lord, you continually clarify your mission.

You are not simply a planner, for the world is full of those. You are a strategic planner. Blessed are the pure in heart, for they shall see God...and blessed are those who focus on the bullseye with sharpshooter clarity, for they shall hit the mark. Each day, today being no exception, fix your eyes on Him, the One who helps you strategically define your prize. He wants to help you devise, revise, and execute an inspired, strategic plan. He will inspire you to inspire others. You, under His power and guidance, will inspire those who appear unable to be inspired. You are gifted with all you need to keep the goal clear, definable, doable, measurable, and worthwhile on a daily basis.

Your Lord Jesus is still laboring in the harvest fields and in the marketplace, accomplishing His Father's business through the power of the Spirit. You get to join Him—and you get paid to do so. You enjoy divine nudging in all kinds of economic climates. Your business partnership with Him makes your work joyous, while for others, it is tenuous and treacherous. Your work is His playground, and you are privileged to enjoy it.

You know that you can do all things worth doing through Christ. You also know that wisdom and faith can walk together down any road and converse with one another in any corner office. You believe that all things are possible, but you still sit down first to strategically plan and order your steps. Yes, the possibilities are endless, and you can accomplish more than you can ask for or even imagine, but a part of you ponders such possibilities through the lens of an inspired strategic plan. Faith comes by hearing, and hearing by the word of God. Hear first, then write out your strategic plan, that a messenger may run with it. Hear, strategize, plan, and write upon tablets. God can supply all of your needs, but will you plan for supply-chain delays? You remain intentionally and cleverly resourceful. You are adaptable and keenly aware, both in times of famine and in times of plenty. Your strategy accounts for it. With a good strategic battle plan, you will not be financially ambushed.

There is a tower or a vineyard or a business out there that you have been called to build. It will serve many. It will be a wonderful place to work and a needed resource for many families. Many other companies and households will benefit from your business, but not by accident. You will be a shade tree for many people because your plan was not just a plan, but an innovative, ever-adapting strategic plan executed with just the right tactics.

Friend, you are called to far more than a rudimentary to-do list. You have been redeemed to supply shade to many. The world can be stifling hot and oh so trying. Strategically plan to provide shade for the weary. Run the race marked out for you and pace yourself strategically. Your future is birthed in part through forethought.

By faith, today I live with Your insight laced with love. May I be quick to see others as You see them. Quicken me today, Lord, with divine insight—on the ready, able to move as You need me to move in order to impact the hearts of those within my sphere of influence. Amen.

DAY 9
Anomal*ous*

My son, do not walk in the way with them,
Keep your foot from their path…
Proverbs 1:15 (NKJV)

Your story is your story. Your story is also part of His-story, so you must be fully you and no one else. You are not unduly influenced by others. You are not susceptible to vain flattery or praise or covetousness. You are discerning and alert to fallacies, faulty advice, and enticements. You discern schemes and lies. You can easily discern falsehoods and the wooing of fruitless conformity.

Your identity is rooted and established in Christ; you are both owned by Him and defined by Him. Your value is quantified by His death on your behalf, not by the accumulation of awards, fame, or material possessions. Your identity is not rooted in ledgers, return on investment, sales penetration, or balance sheets. You are a steward and manager of the opportunities you have been graciously afforded, and you dance to a different tune than those who work only for themselves, apart from the Lord.

Many will sit in the seat of mockers and seek to demean or stall you. Some may even stand in your way and in the way of your dreams. Some may seek to adjudicate you, and others

34

may seek to seduce you with quick riches, but you do not fall into their traps. You meditate on the wisdom that dwells within you and leads you through darkness. You know the safety of a multitude of counselors and the dangers of allowing fads, trends, and distractions to waylay you. You conform to truth, not to this ever-temporary world.

You may love making money multiply. You may love giving money away. You may love investing money. But you are worlds away from being a lover of money. Your motives remain pure, as does your heart. To you, money is but a tool to build something lasting or enhance something righteous or enjoy something joyous. You may enjoy the apparent security of abundance, but you are no lover of money. You are rooted in integrity. What you own will never own you. What you have will never have you. What you invest your time in will at no time destroy you or yours.

You live and work aiming for a higher standard. Your calling is higher; your bar is not low. You never linger only to limbo under mediocre benchmarks that are beneath who you are and who you are called to be. To you, the status quo lacks weightiness and satisfaction. You pursue excellence with excellence. You are an increasingly big thinker and a better worker than ever before. Press on in the stability of single-mindedness. Avoid the instability of duplicity, and deviate not from your co-mission with Christ. You are not a doubter; you are a truster. Persevere. It is never wrong to do what is right. Distractions are deviations, false avenues that will lead you to different goals...or to no goal at all.

Enjoy the freshness of working for the One far above your direct report. Enjoy the challenges of being different as you live and work with uncommon—but higher—standards. Know Who you are yoked with, Who you work beside, and Who you work for. You are His treasured possession. He looks at you and enjoys you and the many efforts you make. Walk and work worthy of His calling. He is your Potter; you are His clay. He has slowly molded you. You are baked in a divine kiln at a specific temperature at a specific altitude for a specific time. He has made you uniquely purposeful. Let your faithfulness be evident and obvious. May you decipher quickly the road that will bottom you out, and may your faithfulness always exceed your bottom line.

––––––––––––––––

Let's "adventure" together today, Lord! Let's journey together to the out-of-the-ordinary—beyond stale norms, beyond lame expectations, and far beyond solidified mediocrity. Can we move in power into newness and freshness, into Your playground that waits just beyond my imagination? Show me how to have fun in You, with You, and for You.
Amen.

DAY 10
Equanim*ous*

...But hospitable, a lover of good, self-controlled, upright, holy, and disciplined.
Titus 1:8 (ESV)

Surely the world of business can be volatile. Markets, rates, pricing, inflation, and resources can at times be unpredictably turbulent. Businesses can dive downward; pricing can soar upward. Markets can plummet. Governments shift, employment rates drop, catastrophes thwart businesses. The winds of change blow, but you remain responsible to family, coworkers, creditors, and your community. Change is at times uncontrollable, but you are self-controlled. Many things are intractable; you are not. When the masses are reactive, you are proactive. When people run, you stand. When people wail, you process. You adapt to change. Outward changes expose your gift of being inwardly capable under duress. People look to you as a barometer of balance. Your faith and confidence steady you when the winds of change become a tempest.

Poise best describes your approach. There is in you no overreaction or overcompensation, but neither will you under respond. You prepare for seasons of change. One man's calamity is your opportunity to be flexible, prudent, and even com-passionate. You need not hide. Look up!

Still waters run deep, and depth is what being a truth seeker has afforded you. When others are steeped in duress, He will make you lie down in green pastures to properly evaluate your next move. Yes, you are calm and composed. As others fret, you compose alternative plans. You are in full control of your faculties, poised to be prudent. There does not exist in you a spirit of timidity or an unsound mind. You are led by love, and you have a rich sense of restraint. Even though the end of all things may be at hand, you are sober-minded and self-controlled. You innately know how to best remain teachable in a crisis. The Spirit of God bears fruit in you, weaving joy and gentleness with your self-control; against such there is no law.

There is a season for everything under heaven, and your faith manifests itself as you properly face seasons of trial. Control of our circumstances and the world around us is but an illusion. You do not fear, for you know the One who is sovereign. He knows you and has numbered the very hairs of your head. He is likewise acquainted with the numbers affecting your business and your coworkers. He honors your diligence, and He prepares and protects you in ways that encourage your trust.

Labor in love as an act of worship, knowing that your Lord ultimately brings about results. Work hard and work smart, both in times of prosperity and in times of duress. Give Him something of integrity and honor to work with, and you will overcome calamity. Remember: your work is worship. He loves and desires your worship. You will have work with which to worship Him. You will not be found begging for bread. Your Provider provides. He also withholds from you when it is best to do so. Trust in Him with all your heart. Lean not on your own understanding; lean on Him. Your lack of understanding of *how* He will deliver you does not negate the fact that He *will* deliver you. Recognize, accept, and acknowledge the things you cannot control, and center yourself in the reality that you are only called to control your own responses under the influence of the Spirit of God.

Your self-control before a storm is stored up to be an abundant resource during a storm. The very self-control needed before a re-cession will prevent you from being without during one. Even in a depression, you would have joy. In hard times and good times, you have joy. Because the joy of the Lord is your strength, you remain strong—both in times of plenty and in seasons of lack.

—————————

Whatever happens today, Lord, may I have poise where there is pressure, peace where there is chaos, and love where there is fear. Ready me for what lies ahead. Together we will set new ways of ministering to this frenetic and fractured world. Help me settle into You and You into me.
Amen.

Day 11
Pi*ous*

*And pray in the Spirit on all occasions with all kinds of
prayers and requests.*
Ephesians 6:18

Your marketplace is not some off-limits playground devoid
of Christ and the ongoing construction of His kingdom. You
know this. Whether subtly or covertly or obviously and
publicly, Christ is actively moving in the marketplace. How
might He enter your arena of commerce?

Through you! When you get on an elevator, you bring the
kingdom. When you make your first call, someone engages
the kingdom. You are a walking tabernacle of the Lord Jesus.
You are pious in every sense of the best-understood meaning
of the word. You are devoted and yes, devout. You are
devoted to bringing the Lord of every lord into the workplace
daily—in your words, in your deeds, in your efforts, in your
labor, and in your love—with the goal of pleasing Him first.

You do this not because of a suggestion or a leaning, but
because is His commandment. At the very least, you go out
into all the world and preach the gospel, using your actions as
a potent, demonstrative sermon. You are a walking embassy
of the Lord Jesus Christ. Where you go, so goes His
kingdom. You are His ambassador, actively moving

throughout your day as His divine consulate. You represent Him at a cash register, a conveyor belt, under a car lift, or in a corporate suite. Your corner office is aligned with the Chief Cornerstone. You sit in His chair, behind His desk, to minister to His employees and His customers. You are His representative. When you speak, you speak with His authority and remain at His bidding.

In fact, your life is not your own. He both ransomed and purchased you, and He positioned you right where you are. Wherever you are, be there. Be there with a wide-awake, fully quickened understanding of your mission. You have work to do, and you do it well. You have people to encourage. You have ears ready to listen to people's pain and weariness. You have a ministry in the marketplace because you are a priest and minister of your Lord, strategically postured to bear fruit that lasts. To encounter you is to, in some big or small way, encounter Christ. Your faith is fully active and engaged Monday through Friday. You know a "faith workout" on occasional Sundays won't get it done. You will not accept spiritual atrophy. You are building spiritual muscle each day. Your faith works out daily and rests on the weekend. On Sundays, you are equipped and encouraged for the next five days of workplace ministry.

You work hard. You work smart. You play hard and enjoy an abundant life, and you operate with a strong business plan. You may know manufacturing, marketing, and your target audience. You may know costs, return on investment, and your shipping needs. You may know all about human resources, employee training, and retention.

But do you know what you need to know about your competitor? Not the shop two blocks over, not the firm uptown, not the broker around the corner, and not the online mega-site, but the competitor that is blinding people to the reality that he cannot deceive, ruin, destroy, or corrupt any business that is marinated in prayer. You work hard, you work smart, and you pray hard.

You are a priest sent into your specific workplace to ensure that your employer, your coworkers, and their families are covered in prayer. Add that to your business plan and you will be about the Father's business, too! You are a priest. A priest tends and keeps. Pray the paint off the walls! Is your workspace not a temple where you worship through the way you work? Is your workspace not an altar where you pray? Are you not the employee starting each day with a covering of prayer from the fullness of your heart, even if under your breath? How much incense—the prayers of the saints—rises to the throne room of grace from your workplace? Ten floors above you, perhaps, important decisions are being made regarding your company and its future. Have you prayed for those in authority? Have you covered your custodians in prayer? Others may have charge over you in the workplace, but you are a spiritual authority in your workplace because you submit to authority.

Wake up, sleeper! Take the on-ramp toward a whole new, fresh way of looking at your job, and you just might see it for what it truly is: a calling. You may be a warrior of Wall Street, but are you a prayer warrior?

―――――――――――

May there be no mistaking me for the spiritually fickle. I am not experimenting with my faith today, Lord. I am resolved to know You and make You known. I declare that I am Yours before I am another's. I am unapologetically devoted to You and Your purposes. I love You.

    Amen.

Day 12
Strenu*ous*

God is our refuge and strength,
an ever-present help in trouble.
Therefore we will not fear, though the earth give way
and the mountains fall into the heart of the sea...
Psalm 46:1–2

Sometimes life and work are arduous. Work can be trying, frustrating, necessary, and unwanted all at the same time. Work can at times be monotonous, spirit-numbing, and altogether draining. Since the beginning, work was meant to be so. Originally, Adam and Eve had a calling; after original sin, they had jobs to do. They had to work strenuously to subdue and survive.

Work is by nature strenuous; jobs can be even more trying. Yes, today we have jobs to do...but are you aware that after the resurrection, we can also embrace our vocational callings? Our callings can require much less effort if we share our burdens with Christ. Do you simply have a job, or are you actively engaged in your calling? Could it be that within your daily work, grateful as you may be for it, lies a yet-to-be-discovered calling?

Perhaps you need an infusion of clarity to reveal your calling, one for you to answer as you fulfill your daily work responsibilities. Purposeful Christ followers should start each day recognizing that within us is an irrevocable calling, regardless of whether we are employed, unemployed, underemployed, or temporarily misemployed.

Consider it pure joy whenever you face trials of many kinds. Tests are good for you. You are a follower of Christ. As such, you are called by Christ and prepared by Him to fulfill that calling. The depth of your necessary preparation is proportional to the scope of your future influence. Two-thirds of the word "God" is "go." If you are going, go deep. Go deep! Ask to be refined and prepared for significant influence in your life and ministry. The deeper you go, the broader your influence and the greater your level of satisfaction.

Pray, and you will soon discover a hidden calling. Pray deeper and more dangerous prayers, and you will soon bask in satisfaction, purpose, and fulfillment—even in your "job."

You know to pray dangerous prayers, whether you choose to do it or not. Who asks the Father to take anything or anyone out of their life that comes between them and God? You do. He is your primary sufficiency. Who first asks for the maturity to handle wealth before pursuing wealth? You do. Who wants to be shown what sacrifice and selflessness truly is? You do. Who longs for patience and is willing to wait on it? You do.

You know that possessions can be good, but it is clear to you that being possessed by your Lord is better. First and foremost, be possessed by Him. Then seek first His kingdom and His righteousness, and all that everyone else seems to be pursuing will be yours. Maturity precedes abundance. You are learning to be faithful in few things, and God is giving you charge over many things. You see things differently than most. You want different things. You are satisfied with less if less has a purpose. You welcome abundance because you have considered the responsibility that comes with it.

48

Who goes to work and puts complaints aside? You do. Who asks to be taught to wait on the Lord? You do. Who asks Him to put to death anything in their hearts or lives that needs to wither? You do. Who asks to be arrested by the Spirit? Who asks God to search their hearts? Who asks Him to test their anxious thoughts? Who asks that any offensive way in them be revealed, exposed, and eradicated? Who asks for love for their enemies? Who asks for critical thinking to replace a critical spirit toward others? You do. You do. You do!

You have a job to do. You approach your work, not begrudgingly, but as an opportunity for further refinement and sanctification. You are grateful for what you have. You also know that seemingly dangerous requests made of your Lord in the context of an arduous job will ultimately lead to a deeper calling.

May His yoke be easy and His burden be light. Cast all your cares on Him; He will never let the righteous fall.

I fear not, Lord. My work is worship. I will face what You need me to face. Help me to work hard when hard work is needed, but help me rest when Your grace is sufficient for the need. Today I choose You and whatever You have for me. Gird me up. You are my glory and the lifter of my head.
Amen.

Day 13
Feroci*ous*

"Do not weep! See, the Lion of the tribe of Judah, the Root of David, has triumphed. He is able to open the scroll and its seven seals."
Revelation 5:5

A nocturnal lion prowls about, seeking to steal, kill, and destroy. He appears ravenous and determined. He wants to render you anemic and lethargic in the workplace—loaded down, unchallenged, and bored. He longs for any and every bit of life within you to be siphoned off by salivating, life-sucking imps. He yearns for you to be an empty shell driven by envy and arrogance. He wants you resentful of those at home who are dependent upon you. Any loathing that eats away at you as you enter the workplace is a trophy in his case and a feather in his cap. He exists to erode your worth so that you flatline and are miserable, sensing no way up or out.

He eats hope for breakfast and faith for dinner. Love he cannot stomach. He wants you tasteless, bland, unattractive, and unkempt.

Great success can be yours in His kingdom if that success intensifies your self-sufficiency and insecurities. He wants what you want if what you want is divisive and inauthentic. He deems it best that you complain about any and all tasks at hand, and he keeps you blind to possibilities for promotion and increased authority. He does, however, advocate prosperity for you—but only if it fosters your demise.

He despises efficiency. He detests any and all synergy and collab-oration that may heighten harmony and effectiveness. He seriously promotes uniformity over unity. He seeks to rip from you any sense of individuality or unique giftedness. He wants you cloaked in mediocrity, draped in pride, and motivated by unearned advancement. He wants you whining and pouting on a regular basis.

But there is another Lion, the Lion of the tribe of Judah. He appears ferocious because He defines ferocity. He seeks to impart life to you. His desire is to graciously gift you and build you up in the most holy faith. He is a mighty Warrior, yet He is also protective and restorative. He abounds with kindness. He loves you and your uniqueness. He wants you as you are, for He created you as such. This Lion sees you as His cub: cute, cuddly, and acutely aware of His presence, purpose, and plan. He wants you to enter the workplace as one enters a temple, expectant of an encounter with Him. He longs for you to serve Him, enjoy Him, and make Him known to those haunted by the enemy, the lesser lion.

You matter to Him. Your efforts are appreciated by Him. He appreciates you and all you do in His name. He is your biggest fan. In fact, He fans into flame the gifts He has placed in you to do your work well. He is your biggest cheerleader. He has placed and is increasing in you a desire to work with excellence. He sees your creativity and your work ethic, and it pleases Him—even if it goes unnoticed by others. You may feel anonymous and unseen, lost in a sea of workers, but this Lion has numbered the very hairs on your head. He has marked you for Himself and His use. No weapon formed against you will prosper, not even the weapons utilized by the lesser lion.

You are wise like a serpent and gentle like a dove. You stand out because you are outstanding. Be who you are. Do what you are called to do. Stand up when others cower. You have eyes to see and ears to hear things to which others are oblivious. Your ear discerns the voice of God. You intimidate the darkness, for within you is the Light of the World. You are strategically placed to take and hold new ground for the kingdom.

You are a loving warrior who matters. Stand your post and be of good cheer. The resurrecting power of Christ lifts your countenance when others fall and quit. People look at you. People will look to you. People are looking up to you. People want Him, the Lion in you, for He who is in you is greater than he who is in the world.

Your Lion, the Lion of the tribe of Judah, walks the corridors and break rooms of your workplace, searching to and fro for those on point, laboring in love before Him. Press on and be his curious cub.

You are quietly ferocious, Lord. Your power is resident in me. What shall I fear? Nothing. You overcame death, hell, and the grave. I trust You. You have my attention and devotion. Nothing is more ferocious than You. Your foe is already defeated. Your enemy is your footstool. I am secure that I am Yours forever.

Amen.

Day 14
Conscient*ious*

Catch for us the foxes,
the little foxes that ruin the vineyards,
our vineyards that are in bloom.
Song of Songs 2:15

If you or your coworkers are not into the details, the devil will be. Little foxes spoil the entire vine. Spoiled vines corrupt an entire vineyard. One small, pesky fox can bring ruin. One seemingly in-significant detail, lazily overlooked, can stymie a project, lose a deal, and ruin a reputation.

You are conscientious. You take pride in your work. It is you who takes a second look, perhaps a third. You prove things right, and you expose things that are wrong. You know the value of excellence. You are not a clumsy, shortcut taker. You aim to do what is honorable. You complete projects and directives as though you're working for an audience of One.

You know well the condition of your flocks. You give attention to your herds. You cannot oversee what you cannot see. You know what you are capable of doing, and you maximize your potential by paying attention to the details. You thrive. You are a hardworking, careful, creative, and thorough success story. You refuse to be entangled in busyness.

Busyness is not good business. You know the shallow, dulled ineffectiveness of busyness.

You, instead, are deeply productive. Many are busy; you are productive. You steward your time, knowledge, and resources in order to produce results. Others dart and dive between distractions, laboring to remember their mission. You set up conscientious boundaries. You keep your focus and remain fruitful. You are conscientious, and your conscience remains clear. You aim to do the honorable.

Nothing is swept under your rugs. You are transparent; you have nothing to hide, and you are ashamed of nothing. You are maskless. You conduct business in an exemplary manner. You will not compromise the inspired mission while tending to specific details, yet you understand that the big vision is a sum total of important details. Your house is in order. Your legalities are in order. Your files are in order. You are in order. Your work reflects your pride in your work. You continue to learn. You remain well-read. You are an asset to your workplace, conscientious and greatly appreciated. You are always an asset, never a liability. Many on the balcony of heaven applaud you. Well done, thou good and faithful servant.

You walk in integrity and run to win the prize. You are trustworthy in a world marinated in deception and honest in a world of insincere promises. You are industrious. You are infused with a spiritual truth serum that guards your tongue. You are a truth seeker, a truth teller, and a truth cherisher. Your "yes" is "yes," and your "no" is "no." You have favor and a good name in the sight of God and man. Who wouldn't want you working with them?

You are an asset to any organization. You are coveted by others, for you are disciplined, diligent, and dedicated. You have integrity, both in times of plenty and in times of lack.

Better is a poor man who walks in his integrity than a rich man who is crooked in his ways. You are upward-thinking and upright in your dealings. You are an uncommon promise keeper.

You admit wrongs. You afford yourself the freedom to fail, and you learn from your mistakes. Oddly enough, your humility exalts you, whereas others 'pride causes them to quickly fall.

You extend abundant grace to others. You keep no lasting records of wrongs, as the plank in your eye hinders you from recording them. You are conscientiously kind. In turn, His kindness leads you to repentance. You, in your unusual way, look carefully how you walk, not as unwise but as wise.

Yes, you know well the condition of your flocks; you give attention to your herds. You know what you have, what you can do, and who can help you, and you are conscientious in the process. Few foxes spoil your vines. You work as unto your Lord, before Whom nothing spoils.

Little foxes will not spoil my vineyard today. Show me, Lord, that little things matter. You are everywhere, including in the details. I submit to the importance of specifics. Even I am Your unique craftsmanship. Show me Your glory in loyalty, thoroughness, and details.

Amen.

Day 15
Slumber*ous*

*In vain you rise early
and stay up late,
toiling for food to eat—
for he grants sleep to those he loves.*
Psalm 127:2

In life, we must put some things to rest, namely our minds, our hearts, and our bodies. Good rest readies us for more productive work, which readies us for good, restorative rest. Working apart from proper rest is a death sentence. Creativity perishes, relationships suffocate, dreams lie dormant, fruit withers, and passion passes away while apathy takes on vibrancy.

In Christ, you learn quickly how to rest. Apart from Christ, you remain restless. Restlessness is an indication of Christlessness. Your mind rests in Him. Your heart rests in Him. Your body rests in Him.

When He is your peace, you rest in peace. Those who rest in peace do so because something has died; when you rest in Him, worry dies, anxiety dies, fear dies, shame dies…and all of their close friends die, too. When you are weary, when you are heavy laden, He gives you rest. He gives Himself to you, and because He does, you rest.

Is it possible that the extent to which your work is worship for Christ correlates to the extent to which your rest is restorative? If so, lazy work yields low-quality rest. Idleness yields no rest at all, only fatigue. Active, worshipful work yields deep, high-quality, restorative rest.

You work hard. You work smart. You worship Christ. You do not worship work. Your identity is in Him, not in your work. You work is something you *do*. Your faith is who you *are*. Do as your Creator does. First, pontificate, adjudicate, delineate, separate, orchestrate, incorporate, and calculate. Then, rest really well.

Rest well, or He will cause you to rest. He will make you to lie down in green pastures beside still waters. Beside still waters, you learn that some holidays need to be more holy days. He is your Creator, and your recreation will not be restful apart from Him. He will help you to sleep. Pray that He helps you to sleep deeply.

Abba, when I am near to You, I sleep as if in Your arms. When You carry me, I sleep best. Carry me that I may drift into peace-filled, sweet sleep.

When I trust You, I sleep best. I trust You; help me to drift off…

When I've served You, I sleep well; free me from serving only myself. I sleep best when I am most childlike; save me from being childish.

I am weary. I need rest. You are my rest. I need and desire You. Still my mind. You keep me in perfect peace when my mind is stayed on You. I choose to minimize fear and rest. I choose to magnify You and rest.

Settle my heart. Let not my heart be troubled. Quiet my flesh. Even the winds and waves obey You.

When I rise, I rise looking for You and to You and for others on Your behalf. Help me to labor in fruitful fields that I may again rest in You. You give sleep to those you love. Do I not love You? May my work warrant Your rest. May my rest, in turn, produce good works. My life is not my own; I was bought with a price. I am Yours. You own me. Care for me when I need rest.

May my life be a sanctuary in which You dwell. May I take sanctuary in You; in You I find my rest. You are my refuge and my hiding place. Do I not dwell in the shelter of the Most High? Will I not abide in the shadow of the Almighty? Will You not abide in me? I choose to rest in You.

Amen.

Day 16
Continu*ous*

The righteous lead blameless lives;
blessed are their children after them.
Proverbs 20:7

Making money is important, but the greedy bring ruin to their households. Families need harmonious time together. When contrast-ed with time, money is a substandard currency. Time is far more priceless than money could ever be. Time with your family yields vastly greater dividends than money. Money is what parents and grandparents spend in large amounts to try to rectify or reverse problems caused by the lack of time they've invested in children and grandchildren. Money vaporizes when spouses fail to invest more than adequate time in one another. Money is no replacement for time together. Making money can certainly cost one substantial time with family members; however, time with one's family costs no money.

Those who overwork may clothe themselves in the rationale that their labor is "for the family," although the time spent overworking is not with the family. That worker may romanticize the extremity of the sacrifice made for the family, yet who exactly is sacrificing? Some who overwork begin with a noble agenda, but in the end, their labor can be a covering for their own personal woundedness. Their emotional accounts may actually be overdrawn. Some toil long and hard in an attempt to satisfy their personal deficiencies. Meanwhile, their families develop a highly personal deficiency of their own.

What makes you so different? In Christ, you know to set boundaries around your family. You establish protective limits guarding them from being ignored. You know deep within that when you ignore those you love, you are being your most ignorant.

You know it's best to work for a living organism rather than an overly ambitious organization. An organism breathes and feels and concerns itself with the well-being of those who serve it. Yes, you know to work for an organism. The culture established and maintained in your workplace is that of prioritizing and nurturing family first. Even your workplace can feel like family. "Pan" means bread. A com-"pan"-y is a group of committed people who labor and break bread together. Members of a company, in the truest sense of the word, share something of value with one another…but never at the expense of each family represented.

You look after not only your own needs but the needs of others. You do not wear yourself out in an attempt to get rich. You trust in your Lord, and your priority is to keep family in its best form and at the forefront of your heart, wherever you are and whatever you do.

What you do, you do for your family. However you do it, there is still something left of you for your family. Your employee benefits benefit your family. Your best you is reserved for them. Your family is unique, beautiful, functional and appreciative of you, your efforts, and your commitment to providing for them.

Take your eyes off your priorities, and something will disappear. Cast but a glance at riches, and they are gone, for they will surely sprout wings and fly off like an eagle in the sky. The *koinonia* love meant for you to enjoy costs you no coin at all. Love your Lord more than you love your work. Love your Lord more than your family. Love your family more than you love your work.

You mean more to those closest to you than you realize. You in-fluence those around you more than you think you do. You are needed by those nearest you more than perhaps you care to admit. You matter. Your presence matters. Wherever you are, be fully there. Actively listen. Tune in. Always choose quality over quantity. Be the friend, sibling, spouse, or parent that others need you to be—and be the one they want you to be.

You matter. One generation proclaims, demonstrates, and models many things to the next generation. Because of you, in your family, there is a continuous passing of a torch that burns brightly for family over and above what happens apart from them. In that kind of family, children are continuously blessed.

––––––––––

You are seamless. Your robe is seamless. You have always been and You will always be. There is no halt to Your grace.

You continuously pursue me. Arrange the priorities of my heart to continuously long to pursue You. I love You.

Amen.

Day 17
Stupend*ous*

Charm is deceptive, and beauty is fleeting;
but a woman who fears the LORD is to be praised.
Honor her for all that her hands have done,
and let her works bring her praise at the city gate.
Proverbs 31:30–31

You provide constructive criticism when others provide only empty, vain flattery. In Christ, you know how to build people up. You know whom to build up, you know when to build them up, and you know in front of whom you should do so. You are an encourager. You are the conduit of the Lord to lift the heads of others.

You recognize what is done right, done thoroughly, and done with excellence. You share sincere praise for others' work at the opportune time. They understand that coming from you, the praise is warranted. You give commendation when commendation is due. Despite differences, grudges, disputes, or opposition, you pro-vide sincere recognition to all who deserve it. You keep personal differences and yet-to-be-resolved conflicts aside as you praise the work ethic of others. You are bigger than pettiness and deeper than manipulation. You encourage with courage.

You acknowledge correct decisions and actions. You identify the use of mature restraint and objective thinking. You give kudos when appropriate. You get it. You get the need to raise up those who serve with and under you. You are a Level 5 leader (Level 6, if there were such a thing). You lead and serve by example. You build up people in earnest.

You are careful not to underestimate a fellow employee's need for affirmation. You know when to recognize the worker and when to recognize the work. You are a wise appreciator of goodness. You can identify those who do well, and you can also identify those who try hard but fail. Beyond results, you see effort. Teaching moments replace criticism, and appropriately so. You can and do reward others for goals reached, quotas met, and contests won. But you help build them up so they do meet their numbers. You initiate their success before they succeed. Your encouragement originates their progress.

You encourage others, both at the city gate and in the most private of contexts. You are a discerning encourager. You bestow honor where it is due. You are honorific in your thinking. Where shame can flourish, you bring preemptive, shame-eradicating honor. Your ex-pressions of appreciation are timely, astute, and healthy. Christ holds all things together, and on many occasions, He uses your encouragement as relational glue.

Your reverence for your Lord presses you into building others up, for He Himself has built and rebuilt you. Those you encourage will, in like manner, encourage and lead others. Your magnanimous encouragement is a genesis for future leaders. When you build up in this present moment, you build up for the future.

You are more open to a word of knowledge or an encouraging word for others than you are for yourself. You provide timely words. Led by the Holy Spirit, your divinely timed words meet needs others know nothing about. You speak to inner, yet-to-be revealed needs. You speak to dimmer and darker pain and wounds. Your comments regarding performance actually perform restorative healing in areas of the soul that are totally unrelated to work. Your encouragement is medicinal. Because you employ truth while encouraging with your words, those words make their way into the marrow of otherwise-discouraged souls.

Bathed in prayer, your career generates encouragement sent from places others do not even know exist. Inspiration is infused into those around you, sent through you from perspectives and locations within the heart of God that cross chasms of need. You can offer up a quick "attaboy" or "attagirl," but there are also times when your words surgically strike to heal wounds mending from the inside out.

You are learning to provide workplace encouragement that is really no work for you at all. Effortlessly, you will offer choice words for choice occasions, words that penetrate human hearts, mend human differences, and catapult people beyond their already-low-level thinking. You are a prophet, prophetically active in a work center that centers on profits. You have been strategically placed among the people you interact with daily. In your God-given sphere of influence, you, in partnership with the Spirit of God, impact "clock watchers" with timeless, eternal implications. The manner in which you do so is compassionate, honest, and revelatory.

Be encouraged. Your encouragement to others is simply stupendous.

Adjectives are great, Lord, but where You are concerned, they fall so very short. If there were millions of words to describe You, millions more would still be insufficient. But for today, You are stupendous. You are far more than I can describe and far above the confines of my finite heart and mind.

All I can say today is that I love You, I honor You, and I worship You. I really do not need anything today but You. Amen.

Day 18
Judicious

The words of the reckless pierce like swords,
but the tongue of the wise brings healing.
Proverbs 12:18

You, like the younger Christ, are growing in wisdom and stature. As your wisdom increases, so too will your stature. As your wisdom in the marketplace trends upward, your ability to solve difficult problems and set strategic plans will likewise increase.

In the power of Christ, you are discovering that wisdom is far more than the aggregation of time, age, and experience. A healthy reverence for your Lord is the beginning of all wisdom and knowledge. He is the source of your wisdom. You, even as the youngest in the workplace, can have more wisdom than those who have far more experience. You are becoming increasingly wise.

The wise are open to instruction. Those who are teachable are also humble. Instruct the wise, and they will be wiser still. Teach the righteous, and they will add to their learning. It is easier to praise another for a job well done than it is to wisely correct another for a job poorly done—or not done at all. You possess the wisdom to correct others in effective ways.

As you continue to grow, you are increasingly able to see things through the lens of biblical truth. You can see when a business owner is really owned by the business. You can see the difference between a job and a calling. You can quickly understand how best to correct another so as to produce greater loyalty rather than alienation. You can correct and build up when others correct and embarrass.

You are sensitive to the power of the tongue. Words can be piercing. Your words create an atmosphere and culture of openness rather than defensiveness. Wisely, you are creating an atmosphere of mutual respect and trust. In that highly functional culture, you can correct— correctly.

You deliver criticism with care. First, you utilize your gift to encourage. Pointing out people's positive attributes first opens their ears to truly hear as they actively listen to you. Your words are laced with the best interests of those on your team.

What you say can be direct and thought-provoking, yet bound in a context of respect. You have wisely cultivated a culture of openness; dealing with mistakes is easier for you than for others. You build up and point out wonderful qualities before you point out errors. Your coworkers will listen to you, for they want to improve. They are team players because you have validated their team play. You will win more games because you say what you mean and you mean what you say. You less frequently need to correct others because you have preemptively and often affirmed them. You manage and lead well.

You have a responsibility to those who work for you and with you. You exemplify excellence and provide a safe environment in which to work, inspiring your teammates to take responsibility for their mistakes. Mistakes to you are affirming teaching moments rather than opportunities to generate hurt, embarrassment, gossip, or division. You employ objective critical thinking and refrain from employing a critical spirit. You employ people with obligations, families, and dreams; they want you to also employ affirming means of correction as you help them grow to overcome their mistakes.

Yes, the tongue has the power of life and death. You wisely consider the ways your Lord corrects you before you correct others. You consider scriptural ways to discipline others because you, as a disciple, have needed that kind of discipline yourself. Your desire to respect your Lord keeps you from disrespecting others. You recognize wrongs as opportunities to grow in wisdom and stature. Judiciously go about your work, mindful of the plank in your eye and the speck of sawdust in the eyes of your teammates. The wise man knows the speck and the plank came from the same tree. Deliver criticism with care. Bring about healing. Let grace abound. Be judiciously wise.

———————————

I thank You today that You did not act justly toward me. I do not want what I truly deserve. I was so lost, so unrighteous. You have been so merciful to me. I thank You that You love mercy, mercy that allows me to walk with You even when I am errant. Thank You for letting me walk with You. May I remain humble and not proud. I love You. Today, I judge not.
Amen.

Day 19
Ambitious

Hope deferred makes the heart sick,
but a longing fulfilled is a tree of life.
Proverbs 13:12

Perhaps you need a getaway, a retreat, to best ascertain how to make advances in your workplace and marketplace. Is your workplace a launching pad for advancement? Does the training you provide prepare people to adequately do their jobs and perhaps advance in responsibility?

Jesus promoted from within whenever possible. He was and is in the development business, developing people and developing His kingdom. He places hope in people, giving them a confident expectation of the possibilities to come.

Many hope for advancement. Advancement may build self-worth in those who otherwise feel stationary. When warranted, you impart genuine hope to others, a hope wrapped around realistic expectations. You fuel their ambition.

Your competitors play checkers. You are a marketplace chess player. You stay many moves ahead, preparing and positioning workers for future positions. You are proactive, not reactive. You are filling needs that have yet to exist while at the same time meeting current needs. You test and train others before they even realize they are being tested and trained. You test their devotion, their confidence, their acumen—sometimes for abilities they have yet to recognize in themselves. You test their willingness to learn. You are a leader who knows to look over the hill and around the bend for what is ahead. You lead from the front, not the rear. You embrace change, not just for change's sake, but for the betterment of your people and your cause.

You are ambitious. Yes, you know when to retreat to ponder your next plan of attack. You lead your company and your coworkers to the Highest Rock. You know when to stretch, test, and challenge, and you know when to take notes. You create future job descriptions based on future needs and technology, and you position people to grow into those descriptions.

You have a keen sense of observation, seeing things others do not, will not, or cannot see. See into your future. Work as unto the Lord and see your way into advancement. It is the Lord who promotes. Get with The Promoter and ask for His eyes to see how to advance people and advance your cause. Take care of them as they take care of you and care for their families.

Be ambitious! Give the Lord something incredibly well-thought-out to bless. He owns the cattle on a thousand hills. He owns the hills, as well. He rains on the hills; He brings light to the hills. Give Him something He would be ecstatic to bless, something strategic, growing, vibrant, and successful, something respectable and mutually beneficial. Worship Him first, then honor Him with your efforts. Then honor those who work to help make it all happen.

Steward His business in a way that reflects well upon Him, and He will bless it. Put His name on the line by truly working in His name, and He will bless it. You are ambitious for your own well-being. You are ambitious for those who are not wired to be ambitious. Your ambition, teamed with wisdom, is enough to advance lives for the glory of God. You ambitiously care. You ambitiously encourage. You ambitiously correct. You ambitiously train and equip. You ambitiously promote those who have proven themselves. You are a priest over those who labor with you and for you. Tend and keep your people. What you do unto the least of them, you do it as unto your Lord.

Your daily approach to life and work does not defer hope in others. Your influence encourages their hearts to remain full, their longings fulfilled as your own. May your heart be grateful and full for the very privilege of leading others. May your humility always exceed your success, and may you experience joy in helping others and fueling their ambition. Because of your ambitious approach to work, you will become a shade tree under which many will come to rest and reflect. Ambitiously serve as a priest and intercessor for those with whom you labor, standing in the gap on their behalf. Your service can yield eternal rewards.

———————————————

I pray, Lord, for consistent courage to press on in life and not be ashamed. I trust You for sufficient courage and zeal to live large. Help me live a life worth dying for. My greatest risk is to take no risk at all. May it be that for me, to live is Christ and to die is gain.
Amen.

Day 20
Bounte*ous*

The generous will themselves be blessed,
for they share their food with the poor.
Proverbs 22:9

You do not truly have something until you are willing to give it away. Those who give nothing away—the miserly Scrooges of this world—may appear to own much but, in fact, are owned by their possessions. The generous will themselves be blessed. Generous people not only give away; they share. Many give and lose touch with the impact of the gift. Those who share continue to participate in the joy of the gift.

You know when to give, and you know when to share. It is the sharing that builds relationships and respect. Give generously and share generously and find yourself blessed.

There is an avalanche of blessing available to you. You are primed to receive this bounty, this flow of goodness. But are you mature enough to receive and handle such a blessing? To whom much is given, much is required. You are increasingly gaining the emotional and spiritual bandwidth required to give and to share generously. You are grasping the true meaning of giving with no strings attached. There is purity in your generosity, an absence of regret in the letting go of your money and belongings. You are not a "white knuckler;" neither are you a hoarder.

You compensate when compensation is warranted. You realize that financial success is impossible without your fellow workers. Reward them appropriately. Be as excessive as is appropriate. Model the bounteous compensation of Christ and walk in the Father's blessing. Compensate people financially, relationally, emotionally, and spiritually. Give your fellow workers the time and resources to earn their compensation. Withhold trophies for participation. Every-one is called to either work or not eat. Bless deserving people.

You provide correct and noble incentives. You articulate clear, attainable, measurable, and repeatable goals. You strategically bless people with weighty projects worthy of additional compensation. You look for opportunities to bless others as they bless you. You look first to your own before looking beyond your people. You build trust as a leader who saves time and money later.

When others see only expenditures, you see investments. You are in the people business, regardless of your product or service, for it is people who make success happen. You invest in those who have already chosen to invest in you and your dreams and career. Your coworkers give of their time and their talents. They labor on behalf of the team every day and, at times, take their work and worry home with them at night. How do you invest in them? You look for ways to secure "win-win" relationships.

You are not a hireling for the sheep. You genuinely care about your flock. Each hire is a new and fresh opportunity. Each exit is a celebration or an opportunity to learn. Yes, you are in the people business. You compensate others by modeling ways to succeed. To work with or for you is to learn how to be successful. You are a demonstrative, walking and talking school for life and business. You share money, time, understanding, business knowledge, and savvy. You are educational and inspirational.

Your efforts are well known. You have developed a witness as a workplace of excellence. As your people advance, so do you. You are being prepared for ever-increasing opportunities to speak into people's lives. You are maximizing the bounteous opportunity afforded you to work as unto the Lord. He has added to your number bounteously. He has subtracted from you when it was beneficial for you. He has divided and organized your resources as you've grown. He will also multiply your efforts and your bounty, to His glory.

Lord, I have all I need. You have fortified me. I pray for aware-ness of and access to Your power and strength. Help me to live like I say I believe. Find me active and fruitful today.
Amen.

Day 21
Zeal*ous*

His disciples remembered that it is written,
"Zeal for your house will consume me."
John 2:17

The marketplace counts on consumers—people who need, want, desire, or crave anything from lifesaving medical treatments to luxury yachts. The marketplace counts, analyzes, forecasts, and leverages the dollars consumers provide. The public psyche is bombarded with daily messages and images that mesmerize and lure the masses toward a mentality of consumerism. If one is good, surely three is better! Barter or borrow, but do whatever is necessary to acquire, "own," or even rent whatever is wanted whenever it is wanted...for to be without, for some, is akin to no longer being.

In Christ, you consume goods because consumption is necessary and unavoidable in order to live. Yet you know that to some "wants" you say no, for to do so is to say "yes" to other needs. You limit or annihilate cravings for short-term desires that would make you a slave to long-term lenders. Sure, you are a consumer, yet you are a prudent one.

In Christ, you are aware of something to which others remain oblivious. You are less concerned with consumerism and more interested in being consumed. Your God is a consuming fire. He will heat you up, refine you, and gently skim off the dross. You are like a milk-based soup: when left alone, you will develop an unappetizing film that needs to be removed. He will skim and stir you into a newer and better version of yourself at the same time that others seek to purchase their way to a new identity through consumption.

You pick up your cross daily, deny yourself, and follow Him. Your modus operandi differs from that of the common man or woman. There is ample room in your life for occasionally going without. You know what it means both to have plenty and be in want, and you find your Lord and His joy in either scenario. You know that being consumed—dying to self—brings new life. "Prune away," you say, for new life comes quickly after the cut. The masses consume and worship at the altar of materialism. You bow your heart to your Lord, a consuming fire. His ways are not our ways. His ways are even more profitable. Being consumed profits you more than a million marketplaces collecting millions.

The Spirit of God is a consumer. He shops in the darkest parts of your heart, seeking to redeem what He has already paid for. He wants to restock your spiritual pantry with compassion for others and a patience you no longer have to wait on.

He seeks to consume you, not against your will, but in keeping with your deepest desires. Placed within you, as if in a time-release capsule, is an ever-present zeal for Him and His will. You want Him and more of Him. You want less of the lesser parts of your sin nature. You can be and are being consumed with a zeal for Him, His ways, His nature, and His life in you. In a culture of consumerism, you are being consumed. You are eaten up with zeal. Zealous are you for a strengthening joy, already paid for and ready for pickup.

Zealous are you for pallets of wisdom and insight, already paid for, recently shipped, and out for delivery. Zealous are you for beautifully wrapped spiritual gifts, already paid for, recently shipped, out for delivery, and soon ready for unwrapping.

Your God is both a consuming fire and a great provider. Jesus Himself was consumed with zeal for His Father's house. Be consumed with a similarly intense zeal. Be a consumer as is necessary. Be not consumed by the mesmerizing influence of a culture being gluttonized into a rabid frenzy.

Be still, and know that He is God. Stand for something and Someone transcendent. Walk worthy of the calling given to you. Run and do not grow weary. Whether stationary or on the move, may you be consumed by your Lord and infused with zeal for Him, His house, and His heart.

_____

How can I not be excited about another day abiding in You, Lord? The possibilities are endless. You are endless. Your goodness is too great to count. You bless me—over and over and over again. Help me bless those who feel empty—over and over and over again.

Amen.

Day 22
Lumin*ous*

Your word is a lamp to my feet
and a light to my path.
Psalm 119:105

Many vocations are uniform specific. Additionally, in order to perform one's duties and be vocationally effective, one may need specific tools or equipment in addition to a uniform.

For example, a miner needs a head lamp. Police officers and security guards need spotlights and flashlights. A lighthouse operator is out of work without a light. Opera singers, rock and roll bands, actors, and comedians all utilize directed light. Professors utilize laser pointers. Surgeons require special lighting, as do dentists. The entire marketplace utilizes light to perform duties. Light provides clarity, safety, accuracy, and precision.

You need light to make decisions regarding your direction. People make pricing decisions, marketing decisions, and manufacturing decisions every day. The marketplace doesn't read palms, tea leaves, or the stars for decision-making, but identifying trends, fads, or shifts in culture can yield profitable results. Making strategic decisions in the light will produce far greater outcomes than will impulsive and reactive decisions made in the dark.

In Christ, you have sense—not just basic common sense, but a flair for soundness, wisdom, and insight. You may use many lights, differing in style, wattage, longevity, and intensity, but you also have access to an additional light. This light, when used effectively, will protect you from yourself, a competitor, or any adversary.

"Thy word is a lamp unto my feet and a light unto my path."

As you familiarize yourself with truth, truth sets you free from fear, greed, pride, and anything else that is petrol for powerfully bad decision-making. Truth, as seen in scripture, illuminates the way so you can avoid catastrophes, pitfalls, and fear-based failure. You enjoy the safety of many counselors—thousands of verses that each serve as scriptural illumination for you, a divine GPS system to guide you to where you need to be.

Clothed in Christ, you must stay dressed for action with your lamps burning. Keep the light on. Keep the Word of God ablaze in your heart. Like Motel 6, the Spirit of God keeps the light on for you. Take advantage of the ancient, irrefutable business wisdom provided by the Ancient of Days. As you do, you will continue to progress toward achieving your goals and objectives without flailing about in the darkness. You use the Word of God as a decision-making flashlight. You use the Word as a protective guardrail on the road to success. You are growing in your understanding, retention, and application of truth, the very truth that sets and keeps you free. You are growing in your ability to hear truth. Your ability to hear the Word of God as it pertains to life and business will soon be exceeded by your willingness to heed divine instruction in life and business. Your ever-increasing success, financial and otherwise, will parallel your meditation of the Word.

You used to worry day and night about making and losing money. You now meditate and ruminate on the Word day and night, your worry decreasing and your bottom line increasing. God speaks to you even as you sleep. He wants you flourishing, successful. He wants to participate in that revelatory process with you, in you, and through you. He loves you and wants you to want Him more than the prosperity He can provide. Never forget: He is a Father. He loves to give you things, but even more, He wants to share life with you, life in which you experience Him and enjoy Him for who He is—not simply for the gifts He gives.

You have a day of work ahead of you. You have a day of worship through work ahead of you. Fill up your tank with truth. Read Proverbs. Enter the marketplace today with a divine flashlight and enjoy the safety of protective guardrails. You just might hear a voice behind you saying, "This is the way, walk ye in it."

———————————

I pray that You will dispel the darkness around me. You are my Light. You are the Light of the world—and my world. Push back darkness and expose every scheme around me today. Amen.

Day 23
Seri*ous*

Be sober-minded; be watchful.
Your adversary the devil prowls around like a roaring
lion, seeking someone to devour.
1 Peter 5:8

Sometimes business calls you out of town into the "unknown." You have been and will be tempted. Some future temptations will be intense; others will be more subtle. Your Lord was tempted during His emptiest moments. You too will be tempted, especially when you are hungry, thirsty, exhausted, vulnerable, alone, and lonely. Know that you will be tempted. Expect as much, for being unprepared can yield catastrophic consequences.

Business can pull you away to the "unknown zones," places where no one seems to really know you. Calling on clients, making presentations, or training customers can place you in situations in which you seemingly become anonymous, invisible, and... unaccountable. In your perceived "unseenness," you actually may be the one who does not see clearly—or at all.

Low to the ground, the tempter prowls, slithering behind you as he waits for you, his prey, to weaken. His strike is sudden, piercing, and deflating. His target, your Achilles' heel, cripples and victimizes you. You are startled, stunned that this could happen to you. You are spiritually paralyzed.

In hindsight, you can see it all clearly. He started weeks ago with the expense account. He progressed to the distortion of your sales figures, and now, he has worn you down, self-condemned and all alone. He was there in the airport, scheming. After lying in wait, he surfaced again in the restaurant. He then backed off just a bit, only to advance again in the hotel bar. He enticed you, as well as others, as you felt the invisible pull of your own "invisibility."

Away from your pack, he senses he almost has you. You will leave the "unknown zone" in one of two conditions: newly devoured or still devoted.

You return home still devoted because you remained properly dressed in your protective armor. Your favorite power suit is your faith. You remain shielded. You were prepared before your business trip ever started. You are wise, bolstered by a sinless Christ. He is your Potter; you are His clay. He is molding and shaping you into the best and strongest version of the new you. You are not putty in the hands of the prowler; you are clay in the hands of your Potter. You are never alone. He will never leave you nor forsake you. He is an ever-present help in time of trouble. When you are most fatigued, He is your strength. When you are most hungry, He is your sustenance. He travels with you and in you. You abide in Him, and He abides in you. You are enveloped. He is omnipresent. He is in every airport, every hotel, and every hotel bar.

You know when to be serious and sober-minded. You know when to remain guarded. You remain in Him and in His Word. Serious implications and consequences await those who allow themselves to wither on the vine. You run with your pack of encouragers, and you move about as you seize good opportunities. No weapon formed against you will prosper. You will overcome. You are prepared in advance for temptations to come, and you are strengthened. You overcome by the name of Jesus and the blood of the Lamb and the word of your testimony. Worship is your weapon. Your worship in the "unknown" insulates you from a cold, frigid heart.

You wield a doubled-edged sword that cuts both ways. Stay in the Word. Your armor covers your front side. Who defends you from behind when prowling and slithering temptations seek to spiritually cripple you? He who walks with you and has your back. At times, He will even carry you.

Be wise. Work smart. Rest well. Lean on and lean into your Lord, for He knows the power of temptation when you are tired, empty, and vulnerable. Enter the "unknown zones" knowing exactly who you truly are and to Whom you truly belong. You will remain devoted. You will not be devoured.

_____

Keep me at the ready, Lord. I pray for discernment. Tend to me and keep me aware of my surroundings. I pray for serious eyes that see serious needs, though they may be hidden and shadowed. Help those in need of serious breakthroughs.

Amen.

Day 24
Alacri*tous*

*...Rendering service with a good will as to the Lord and
not to man, knowing that whatever good anyone does,
this he will receive back from the Lord,
whether he is a bondservant or is free.*
Ephesians 6:7–8 (ESV)

You have the ultimate Servant within you, and He needs to be let out.

"The Son of Man did not come to be served, but to serve, and to give His life as a ransom for many."

Your key to quality customer service necessitates that you serve the right Master. You know that if you please Him, you will likely please others. If you please Him but fail to please others, you are not discouraged, understanding that some are just never pleased. You are accommodating, respectful, and gentle. You embody poise under pressure. When some choose agitation, you choose poise. Your levelheadedness yields great patience.

Your good heart, will, and intentions commingle with your great focus on exceptional service. You care, and because you care, little foxes fail to destroy your crop. You pay attention to detail, and you pay attention to people. For you, people are not numbers. People are not projects. People are the conduit through which your Lord provides for you. Please Him and prosper. Do exactly what you say you will do. Do it when you say you will do it and in a manner as promised, if not better, and see your barns filled to overflowing and your vats brim over with new wine. You have integrity, and integrity produces a harvest of satisfaction. You exceed the expectations you have committed to provide and, because you do, you are an exceptional exception. You render service with goodwill. You render your service first unto Him and then to man.

Your care for others secures the loyalty of many. Their devotion provides additional

customers for you. You have and are continually building a good witness before those who work with and for you. You represent your Master well.

When others look for the path of least resistance, you resist the urge to compromise. Well done. It matters. You matter. Your efforts are pleasing and acceptable. A wise person welcomes instruction, and you welcome instruction and correction. You are quick to make corrective changes and to create solutions so others can go about their business. You follow through when others come up short, and you complete what others fail to finish. You make a ministry of finishing. When it seems as though everything is falling apart, you hold on, for He holds all things together. Your thoroughness is noticed. Your customers appreciate your quality, while most others fixate on quantity. You are compensated more because you go the second mile. You have received blessings back from the Lord because He sees, He knows, and He appreciates your appetite for excellence.

Your second-mile mentality merits a reward. You know how to make an impact. You know how to set a new standard. Influencing others and setting the bar higher is noble.

Standard setters lead from the front; they never follow from the rear. You find honor in hard work. Additional positions and responsibilities will be entrusted to you because you devote yourself to things to which the Spirit of God is devoted.

May you discover great satisfaction as you satisfy others' realistic expectations. You can do all things through Christ who strengthens you. Not only can you do all things, but you can do them in an exemplary manner. You do not seek credit or affirmation; you simply do the right thing. You quietly make it your ambition to live a quiet and peaceful life. You desire to think on all that is true, noble, right, pure, lovely, admirable, excellent, and praiseworthy. You bring your best gifts before your Lord. Integrity is fleshed out in your work, and it is commendable. Well done, thou good and faithful servant.

Show me today, Lord, what I need to see quickly. Sensitize me to what needs tending to quickly. Keep me timely and ready, in season and out. I pray to be responsive, as You have, on so many occasions, been for me.
Amen.

Day 25
Unpretenti*ous*

Let the favor of the LORD *our God be upon us,*
and establish the work of our hands upon us;
yes, establish the work of our hands!
Psalm 90:17 (ESV)

The Spirit of God can and does light upon you like a dove. He can and does anoint you to work and represent Him well. He empowers you to do and accomplish things beyond your current knowledge and experience. He reveals Himself through your results, results that without Him would be vain and unimpressive. Yes, He can and does light upon you like a dove, bestowing upon you what you lack in order to do even greater works than Christ.

Not only does His anointing rest on and well up from within you; His favor rests on you, as well. Because of this, you can rest in Him. He does not show favoritism, nor does He favor you above others, yet His present and active movement in and through your life yields for you an unmerited favor with others. You walk in, work in, and move about in the favor of God. Doors will open for you that do not open for others. Opportunities are afforded you. Misfortune does not always befall you, though it might befall another. You wear the favor of God like a custom-fitted suit. It fits you because you find serving God and others in His power and for His glory most fitting for you. Grace is yours in abundance. What you do in the favor of God is more efficient, less wasteful. There is, at times, an effort-lessness to what you do because He has gifted you to do things that He Himself is helping you do. There is an elegance to your work that impresses others without them really knowing how you do it. That favor lights upon you as you pray for others, pleading for humility.

You have been given favor by God and a good name in the sight of man. You lean not on your own understanding. There are not many instances when you do not acknowledge Him. You

are a billboard for unmerited favor and grace. Receive it; believe it. Do not complicate it. It just is. Leave it to Him. In Him you live and move and have your being. His favor allows you to have authority. In His authority, you do not need to yell or raise your voice. You have the authority and the anointing and the favor of God, yet you are unpretentious.

When someone hires you or retains your services, they retain the services of the Spirit of God. To engage you is to engage the participation of the Lord on your behalf. You continue to decrease, and He increases. You die to self, and the power of the resurrection comes in like a flood.

See yourself differently and experience different results. Do not condemn yourself, but lower yourself. Go low to achieve much. Go low to receive more. Give up the seat of honor at the table and receive honor. Humble yourself in the sight of the Lord, and He will lift you up. Lift up Christ in word and in deed, and He will draw all men unto Himself.

The favor of God rests on you because you need not be His favorite. You have a greater affection for serving your fellow man, demonstrating the wisdom and grace of God for His glory and not your own.

He has established the work of your hands. He prepared good works for you to do long before your awareness of such works. He has also provided the space and the compensation to do them in the marketplace and the sense to know that it is not just you who does them; it is Christ in you. Every day is Take-the-Holy-Spirit-to-Work Day. He favors you. He affords you respect and esteem.

To whom much is given, much is required. Walk worthy of the calling. Walk mindful of the Dove. Enjoy the divine partnership; you are the vessel, and He is the oil. Pour, pour, pour into this all-too-squeaky world. Many tin men await you this week. You walk in the favor and anointing of God.

Father, I acknowledge Your favor on my life. I am aware of Your presence in my life. I, in no way, will ever pretend to understand or deserve Your anointing. Yet You remain with me and upon me for Your purposes. I do not credit myself, but I do speak the truth. I invite You to continually use me as You will, for Your glory and for Your honor, now and for always.
Amen.

Day 26
Valor*ous*

In all toil there is profit,
but mere talk tends only to poverty.
Proverbs 14:23 (ESV)

Your success in life and in your workplace is predicated, in part, on what you say and how you say it...along with what you don't say. You know when to speak and when to guard your tongue. Others speak, only leading themselves to ruin. Your words preserve life. You know the power of the tongue to bless or curse. You are careful with words.

Talk is no substitute for toil; in all toil, there is profit. In a world focused on making profits, talk is often cheap. You can never afford to replace effort with talk. People who work little get nervous. Nervous people talk too much. When words are many, sin is not absent. You discern the difference between speaking much and saying nothing and speaking little and moving mountains. You have an instructed tongue.

Like your Lord, you can preach a sermon with very few words. You can go to work, pick up a towel and a basin, wash feet, and leave, having communicated a far greater message than you would have merely talking about cleanliness. You are a doer. Your faith is not without works. As you consider using fewer words, you will find that you communicate more. Too much talk is an attempt to create a façade behind which there is very little content. If you need attention, work. You say more when speaking less. People are more attentive when you speak out of the abundance of a pure heart.

Your words are well chosen, flowing from a well of productivity. Your words are creative and uplifting, as is the quality of your work. You were likely hired to work first and talk second, so work with all your heart.

Compared with others, you seem a bit odd. It seems odd that you speak to people's faces and not behind their backs. You remain willing to confront and face rather than to talk and hide. It's odd that people have long since given up on coming to you to gossip. You find it inferior to speak ill of a superior. It is clearly obvious that you are running a race while others are running their mouths.

Yes, where words are many, sin is not absent. Talk can often be cheap, but too much of it gets really expensive, leading to poverty. Work for the glory of God and shine like a star in the universe as you hold out the word of truth. Do everything without arguing or complaining. Your words are choice and often premeditated and strategic. When you speak, you speak with authority—and people listen. You are not tuned out before you speak, nor are you ignored after you speak. You are discretionary. You have set a guard over your mouth. You possess the power to bless. You speak without vengeance. Your speech is beneficial.

There is no "try;" there is only "do." "Trying" is too often for those who just talk about being productive. Those that do as they say accomplish more. You are not nervous; you are valorous. Many see valor in your efforts. In the face of many accolades, you embody humility. You have few illusions concerning your work, your role, or your results. You are equipped, prepared, and confident. You can courageously deal with challenges from which others shrink. Your fearlessness speaks volumes. You speak often and with clarity and influence, but only when it is an improvement on silence.

Yes, your words are choice. Never will there be an autopsy for your dreams, for you work toward them rather than talking them to death.

Are you not my King? Have I not access to Your courts? Have You not knighted me? Do I not wield Your two-edged sword? Send me, Lord, to bestow valor on the shamed and valor on the brokenhearted and valor on the compromised. Send me in Your power to bring honor to the dishonorable, in your Name.

Amen.

Day 27
Tenac*ious*

Wealth gained hastily will dwindle,
but whoever gathers little by little will increase it.
Proverbs 13:11 (ESV)

Instant gratification seems to take too long in this day and age. This world grows impatient even while pursuing patience. For many, an overwhelming, frenetic confusion thwarts a deeper understanding of true success. Many want to hurry their way to the acquisition of influence and profit, impatiently waiting for a windfall that never comes. Their shortcuts cause them to lose their way in the attempt to reach their objectives. They desire immediate gratification, and they cannot find it fast enough. Their lives and careers are sprints; yours is a fruitful, gratifying marathon. They burn out. Through your endurance, you gain life. You understand the purpose of time and its role in maturity, growth through experience, and the accumulation of wealth.

Things hastily gained are often quickly lost. Things quickly acquired are appreciated less than those earned over time. You are an earner. Gather what you are going to gather, little by little, and through your diligence, it will increase. You understand compounding value over time. As you steadily gather respect, favor, and wealth, each will gradually increase.

Your patience is not only a discipline or a personality trait; your patience is a fruit of the Spirit. Patience, for you, is not as much an "it" as it is a "He."

Plow your plat and plod along, sowing good seed, and you will reap a harvest. Gather up the Lord's increase. Do not forget those who wish to glean from you. From your harvest, the poor glean a share. You are gleeful, never wasteful, and you remain useful. You know how to actively wait upon the Lord; as a result, you ultimately soar. Some are diligent, but your diligence is tenacious. Your ways are not unlike those of the ant. Your ways are wise. You prepare your bread in summer, and you gather your food in harvest.

Many prepare to plan. They get ready to commence. They launch, only to soon initiate a new start…and then only to begin again in a different direction. They want to go viral and sustain an unwarranted immortality. They soon rebrand and sprout new leaves but never become a tree.

You are an oak of righteousness for the display of His splendor. Many sprint like a leopard, only to soon tire. You make a ministry of finishing while others make a lifetime of restarting. You run to win the prize to which you are called heavenward in Christ Jesus. You press on to win the goal. His glory is in your finish. He started a good work in you, and He will carry you on to completion until the day of Christ Jesus.

Stay the course laid out before you until you are called to a new course by your "Caller." Become an expert in a world of wannabe amateurs. Become your best. Continue to learn and grow. Become an authority and work with authority. Make mistakes and leverage them while others deny their mistakes and run away.

This world's mentality is temporal. Yours is eternal—and you affect eternity. You worship the Alpha and the Omega. You appreciate the fullness of the infinite facets of God. You know the necessity of a good start, but you experientially understand the fullness and satisfaction of a good ending. You do well when you embrace consistent devotion. You remain fruitful when you continually abide in Him. You will continue to plunge into the depths of a true, insightful friendship with Christ and, as a result, He will broaden your influence. Your Potter is a Plotter. Stay the course. Do not grow weary of doing good, for in due season you will reap, if you do not give up.

Lord, You know how to wrestle. Teach me to wrestle, as well. Teach me to agonize over the wayward and the lost. Show me what it is to weep over the aimless. Help me to wrestle not against flesh and blood. Light upon me with Your Spirit, that I may see Your victory on behalf of prodigals.
Amen.

Day 28
Aur*ous*

Whoever is slack in his work
is a brother to him who destroys.
Proverbs 18:9 (ESV)

Slackers help destroy companies, killing the dreams of those who own them and those who work for them. A slacker is a thief and a fool; a slacker acts like family to the one whose mission it is to kill, steal, and destroy. A slacker's activity produces nothing more than fool's gold.

You are not a slacker, nor do you enable the slacker. You are wise. You have a different value system. Placed upon you is a mantle, a high calling that requires the assistance of God to answer. Your work is valuable, like gold; it is aurous.

You are golden. You are of a golden age, marked by valued achievements realized through honest gain. The mindset of a golden age is that of peace, harmony, prosperity, and stability. You are a "golden age" worker for Christ. You have an "aurous-ness" about you. You are growing ever closer to Christ. He no longer calls you His servant, but rather, "friend."

Gold, as an element, is not the result of any chemical reaction. It is created by God and found in nature in its rawest form. In that respect, you are like gold, for you are created by

God to be naturally you and no one else. Like gold, your level of purity can be measured. You are increasingly growing in purity, for you are being sanctified. Your heart is becoming ever purer and more focused. You know that "blessed are the pure in heart, for they shall see God."

You may have started out in the rawest of forms, like an oddly shaped gold nugget discovered in a riverbed outside Eden. Yet you and your work are being purified, shaped, and buffed, not unlike the paved streets in the paradise to come.

You, like gold, are a work in process. In fact, your work is a work in process. You are gaining knowledge, efficiency, and expertise. Expect much out of your partnership with your Lord. Does He not call you to do even greater works than He? Is He not helping you in the process? Has He not promised you the quintessential Golden Age? Is He not your partner in achievement, helping you make peace and harmony as you succeed? Is His active involvement in your life not golden?

The purity of your work is exemplary, like gold. You deliver and do not disappoint. You can be counted upon. You walk and work in "aurous integrity." You are humble and not prideful; but you have an appropriate pride in your work. Should you not be proud of your efforts? Others provide you with earnest accolades; are you not deserving? Is there any reason you should not be proud of what you produce? Is there not honor in your work, your efforts? If you can only love others to the extent you love yourself, can you not appreciate your work for what it is, as well? Can you not build yourself up in the most holy faith—without arrogance? As "golden" as you are and as "golden" as your work is, appreciate yourself in Christ. You are the King's kid! Should you not see yourself as special? Do you not have something of worth to contribute? Is anything forbidding you from feeling confident and whole?

Value yourself, for you are nothing but an asset to any workplace. Like royalty, you are golden.

In fact, you are part of a priesthood of all believers—a royal priesthood with golden crowns and full access to the King's palace, courts, banquet tables, libraries, and gardens. Yes, you are golden, aurous. Let the scripture give you license to appreciate yourself for who you are going and growing to be. You can run boldly to the throne of grace at any given moment, for you are an heir and joint heir of the King, fully inheriting eternity and every good and perfect gift that comes from the Father above. You are of a golden age. You are not a slacker. Awaiting you are many crowns. Well done, thou good and faithful servant/friend.

I am wealthy. I have much gold, pure gold, for I have You. Your lampstands are golden, Your censors are golden, Your streets are golden, Your sunsets are golden. Who am I that You are mindful of me? You are my worth and my wealth. To me, You are priceless. Besides You there is no other. I stand in awe of You. Your grace is my sufficiency.

Amen.

Day 29
Preci*ous*

"No one can serve two masters, for either he will hate the one and love the other, or he will be devoted to the one and despise the other. You cannot serve both God and money."
Matthew 6:24–26

In Christ, your value is priceless. You were bought at an inestimable price, ransomed from the darkness and brought into His marvelous light. Your life is not your own. Your value is as measureless as the infinitude of eternity. When He bought you with His blood, your worth entered a state of incalculability. You are His treasured, precious possession.

There is no price index or market analysis that can chart your worth. All you know is that one day, you possessed a righteousness as filthy as oily rags. Then, on the day of your salvation, Righteousness purchased you. You are now possessed by Him. One drop of the blood of Christ shed on your behalf propelled you into the realm of pricelessness. Your worth is permanently tied to that index. You were very low when Christ bought you, and He will hold you for the long haul. Your worth determines who you are; your worth is your identity. Your identity is rooted and established in the finished work of Christ.

Christ, though once dead, is now alive. He is real, knowable, personal, and accessible. He not only loves— He *is* love. He experiences emotions, like jealousy, over you. He feels. He is an animated, loving Master.

The value of a dollar can fluctuate hourly. Its value is ever changing. Fickle foreign markets, supply chains, and inflation can all have a volatile bearing on the value of a dollar. Any aspect of currency value can be calculated at any given time. Your currency was created by man, for man. It is temporary. One day it will be replaced. It has a unique ability to become a master. Master money, or it may master you. Your identity—and that of others—can become rooted in the possession of money or the lack thereof. If it does, your perceived self-worth will go up and down like a roller coaster. Root yourself in money, and your foundation will rot.

Idols are made by the hands of man. They have no ability to care for or empathize with you. Idols are objects that are worshiped. People become like what or whom they worship. If you worship money, you will sense at times that you are valuable and at others, that you're worthless. Idol worship leaves one with an ever-fluctuating, polarized sense of self. There is nothing wrong with money; it is the love of money that is the root of all evil. Love money and fan the intensity of the jealousy of God. Flee from idols! You cannot love both God and money. You cannot serve both God and money. Love your Lord.

Pricelessness cannot be equally yoked with a devalued dollar. Eternal life cannot be equally yoked with a temporal dollar. Your mortality has put on immortality. You operate by different standards of weights and measures.

You pursue the kingdom first, and the King provides for you. Those who seek the provision first will likely miss the King. Seek the King because He is the King, not merely for what He can do for you. Seek Him, that He may be found. He is enough. He is more than enough.

Work at whatever you are doing with all your heart, the very same heart with which you love Him, and you will succeed. Live your life with depth. Make Christ your anchor, and drift not into materialism, consumerism, or any other "ism." Be His, and He will be yours.

Is this land not filled with idols? Many bow down to the work of their hands, to what their own fingers have made. Many pay homage to vain idols, forsaking their hope of steadfast love.

But you have depth. May your love abound more and more in knowledge and depth of insight.

———————————

I could pursue money, but how brief would be its satisfaction? I could pursue riches, but how briefly would it satisfy? I could pursue financial security, but how briefly could I trust in it? If I am precious to You, then I will pursue You, the only One who imparts true, lasting worth. I see You as precious, just as You see me as precious. If You, Lord, are my primary pursuit, I am confident I will find myself resourced and ready to make You known to others.

Amen.

Day 30
Industri*ous*

Surely you can dream, far beyond even the American dream, if only for a moment.

One weekday in the not-too-distant future, from the market's opening bell to its closing bell that afternoon, an odd but welcome spiritual tectonic plate shift takes place. There is a moving of heaven to earth whereby all things are revalued and reevaluated. The Spirit of God hovers over the marketplace, drawing all workers to Himself. People ask questions far removed from the typical status quo. They feel different, and they inquire about it. They curiously declare an openness to their otherwise-guarded hearts. From the elevated C-suite to the mailroom below, employees gather to discuss an aching in their hearts for God. They know what they want but grasp for a way to seize it. While quite aware of their sin, they are also strangely warmed.

Needing help understanding this Presence in their office or factory or classroom, they look for answers. In your workspace, they look for you. Seeking you out, they find you not stunned or equally curious. They find you centered and prepared. This particular day is no spiritual ambush for you. You have longed for it, begged for it, prayed for it. You, the priest in your workplace, have believed by faith and yearned for a marketplace revival. Your heart's cries were like fragrant incense laced with love. This awakening you longed for is now at hand. You picked up your spiritual weapon and stood at your post, ever waiting and ever faithful. You and others prayed Him in. You and others created a magnificent throne of praise in your workplace for Him to be seated upon. His Presence, always there, day in and day out, is now palpable, weighty, and glorious.

You now know why you were called to this place at this time. It is the perfect *"kairos"* time, a season in your life never to be forgotten. You stood in the gap, and now you close the gap as you lead others, one by one, to Christ. The sea of forgetfulness rises to unprecedented levels as a wave of confessed sin roars in with a new tide of repentance.

You remain anointed, empowered as you share the Word, lay hands on the sick, and lead the aimless to Christ. You are centered in the will of the Father—for the glory of the Son and in the power of the Spirit. You, an eyewitness of Christ's presence and activity in your life, are now an eyewitness of a radical, unprecedented transformation in the marketplace.

You can now see even clearer. The holy huddle of prayer you formed years ago with fellow workers was a conduit of grace and faith for others. A volcanic outpouring of God's presence had been nearing eruption for years. He called you to your place of labor for more than a paycheck. He called you there with a higher calling, one requiring love and patience, and He saw you as His faithful child and used you to hold back the darkness.

All these months and years you have been ambitious—not just for personal advancement, but for the advancement of the kingdom. You have labored long and hard, but you have also labored in love for others. God has blessed you with His favor, but you wanted favor for others more. You were generous, luminous, and zealous, and your Lord honored your honorific prayers for others. You are a workplace priest fulfilling your high calling with a lowliness embraced by few others. You have served your Lord where He has placed you, and you have served Him by serving the least among you.

This is no spiritual ambush that catches you off guard; this is the day and season for which you have longed, worked, and waited. Your vigorous quest for revival has been realized. You and The Greatest Revolutionary in the history of creation have partnered to see not a second historic industrial revolution but a revolution within industry.

Well done, thou good and faithful servant!

"Turn to me and be saved, all the ends of the earth! For I am God, and there is no other."

I truly do not know what You will bring to pass around me. Yet, Lord, would it not be errant of me to believe You for only a little? I desire to believe You for the colossal—and for revival. I choose to believe and hope and trust, not in a small, abbreviated version of You, but in the fullness and grandeur of Your glory.

Help me think and pray big, that I may not remain a small, abbreviated version of my current self.

Amen.

Gary Hewins is the lead pastor of Community Bible Church in the beautiful mountains of Highlands in Western North Carolina. Across the world, people of many nations appreciate Gary's passionate and unique delivery as he rightly divides the word of truth.

With more than twenty-five years of experience as a communicator and consultant, Gary uniquely presents the Word of God in a way that is understandable, challenging, and applicable. His teaching spurs others on to grow in maturity in Christ, discover God's calling on their lives, and impact the world for Him.

Gary holds a Doctor of Ministry degree from Gordon-Conwell Theological Seminary in Boston, Massachusetts. He also serves as the president of Lifepoints Corp., a consulting and training ministry and retreat center for vocational and lay Christian leaders worldwide. Home base for Lifepoints is the tranquil Five Apple Farm in Highlands, North Carolina. (www.FiveAppleFarm.com)

9 798999 320704